Saved & S.E.X.Y.

For the Almighty God

Tiffany D. Taylor

Scripture taken from the NEW AMERICAN STANDARD BIBLE®, Copyright © 1960, 1962, 1963, 1968, 1971, 1972, 1973, 1975, 1977, 1995 by The Lockman Foundation. Used by permission.

Scripture taken from the New King James Version®. Copyright© 1982 by Thomas Nelson, Inc. Used by permission. All rights reserved

All stories in this book are true.

Cover Design by Tawana Cox – ETC Studios, Houston, Texas

Assistant Editor – Tasha V. Mount – Howard University, English Literature

Saved & S.E.X.Y. for the Almighty God

Copyright © 2009 by Tiffany D. Taylor

Houston, Texas 77000

ISBN 978-0-578-03040-1

Published by Tiffany D. Taylor

www.lulu.com

All rights reserved. No portion of this book may be reproduced in any form without the written consent of the Publisher, except by a reviewer who may quote brief passages in a review to be printed in a newspaper, magazine or journal.

Version 1

Printed in the United States of America.

Saved & S.E.X.Y.

For the Almighty God

Tiffany D. Taylor

This book is an inspirational memoir exemplifying how women who are called by God and choose to live a saved life can overcome insecurities as they acknowledge, accept and embrace not only their outer, but also their inner beauty. Saved and Satisfied, Saved and Encouraged, Saved and Xenoglossia (Speaking in tongues), and Saved and Yielding- For the Almighty God was written to encourage and inspire all women striving to live Saved and S.E.X.Y.!

Saved & S.E.X.Y.

For the Almighty God

Tiffany D. Taylor

Dedication

I would like to dedicate this book to my son Kevonn and daughter Sarai,

who have given me many reasons to seek the guidance of God

in which every situation worked out in our favor.

To God be the Glory.

Contents

- Acknowledgements
- Introduction
- I Am
- Chapter 1 – Saved and S.E.X.Y. - For the Almighty God
- Chapter 2 – Getting to a Place Where Your S.E.X.Y. Can Be Used by God
- Chapter 3 – S.E.X.Y. Women in the Bible
- Chapter 4 – Living Saved & S.E.X.Y. Single
- Chapter 5 – Living S.E.X.Y. & Married, S.E.X.Y. & Divorced
- Chapter 6 – Saved, S.E.X.Y. & Honorable in This World
- Daily Prayers and Dedications

Acknowledgements

I would first like to thank my Lord and Savior Jesus Christ. As the saying goes, I would be nothing without Him. However I would like to take it one step further and say, With Him I am everything.

I would like to thank the prayer warriors who continued to cover me while I was under attack during my transition from grace to Glory.

I would like to thank my two children for being my two children and not allowing me to sleep and sometimes eat…but always giving me a reason to stay on my praying knees. Without the motive, there would be no motivation and without motivation, there would be no action. Without action, there would be no reaction- thus in Christ I would have never grown.

Thank you.

I would like to thank my Aunt Geraldine "Geri" Brown (may she rest in peace) for embracing me early in life and modeling how a *Saved and S.E.X.Y.* woman should be. Because of you I know that each person's duty on this earth is to make a difference in the lives of others. This journey is not ours. We can't take it with us when we die, but we can leave it for someone else to travel. Praise God for the Aunt Geri's in this world!

Thank you, Grandmother, for being the rock in this family. Not only the sole provider many times, but the strong woman that never allowed the wind to sway you. You are an inspiration to my soul! I love you and I thank God for all of your teachings.

I would finally like to thank the rest of my family and friends for supporting me and loving me through many years of joy and pain, peaceful times and struggles, the many sacrifices and the much deserved praise.

May the grace of God be with you always.

Introduction

As I look back over my life, I can truly say that I have been tried and tested and tried and tested again. I've come to realize that each person's life within itself is a series of untold stories, painted pictures and hidden treasures. I find it fascinating that as we live our lives we are given choices that will either benefit or hinder us as we, as human beings, blindly walk paths of the unknown. However when we revisit our past, we see that from day one God was always available to guide, counsel and shield us on our journey. It's not until we are able to understand that the many hills and dead valleys we've traveled carrying unbearable loads as we stumbled forward, could have been a little easier and much lighter if we would have been wise enough to just yield and let God's hand take ours. Because of this our life story becomes many. All the wrong turns and setting up camp on enemy territory; we either learn early that **"God is the way, the truth and the life"** or we learn late. Regardless, we will learn.

In my time here on earth, it's taken me some time to understand my own story. Searching for answers and truths, while blindly wandering in a foreign land for many years, had me empty without meaning. Much insecurity plagued my overall being holding me back from receiving the wholeness of Christ. As I peel back layers and layers of past experiences, I now understand that I was called by the Almighty God from my mother's womb.

My life has a new meaning these days. I've embraced my inner beauty and allowed God to reveal the hidden treasure that has been buried deep within me! The devil had me thinking that my self worth was measured by my physical beauty and what I can obtain in *this* world by manipulation. You see the enemy led my life for many years and I had no idea that in a general sense I was actually being pimped to the world; But God has opened my eyes to see that He is the creator of all things. He blesses all of us with so many different gifts and attributes that we all may be used in some way, shape or form to bring people closer to Him. There are many paths we may happen to choose but regardless of which we travel, we are to utilize everything God has blessed us with.

One might say that in every life there is a story to tell; but I say, in every story that is told, there is life.

I AM!

A Message from God

Actual words spoken by God in a dream. I was told to wake up and write…

I am says the Lord!

I am.

I am says the Father…

I am.

I am says the Son…

I AM!

I am says the Holy Spirit…

I am.

I am your friend, I am your counselor.

I am your teacher,

I am your…preacher.

I am your doctor, your lawyer, your sister, your brother.

I am your judge.

I am your provider.

I am your ALL MIGHTY GOD!

I am…your desire.

I am your peace in the midst of your storm.

I am the lift you feel when you say, "I can't go on!"

I am the voice you hear that whispers to your heart,

I am the moon, the sun, the light and the dark.

I AM!

I am the rain,

I am the lightening.

I am the thunder…

I AM!

I am the flowers,

and wind that blows through the trees.

I am the force that has power to calm the roaring seas!

I AM!

I say…I am.

Hear me my children this day.

I am the laughter that fills the mouths of children as they play.

I am,

the joy of new life,

I am…life.

I am…everlasting life.

I am your healer.

I am your redeemer.

I am

your rock on which you build,

on which you stand,

and sit,

and lay…and cry,

and cry…

and cry…

and…cry.

I am that hand that guides you.

I am that strength that moves you.

I am

the tears you cry as you lift your voice to the sky.

I AM.

I am

the doctor, my sister- I have spoken…I AM THE FINAL SAY.

I am

the cellmate, mother- your son will be okay.

I am

the strong arm, my brother- I will bring your wife back home.

I am

your shelter, my hurting teen- you've strayed…it's okay come on home.

I am

that bum on the street!

…Don't you see me?

I am

that little old lady needing help across the street.

I am

the bird that flew on your window pane.

(laugh) – yeah I know,

You didn't think birds flew in the rain.

Children, Children, Children!

I am your Sheppard!

I look out in my fields,

and search for one of my own kind…

Ohhhhhhhh but all I see is the blind leading the blind!

I am

your covering.

I am

your favor…

I am your grace.

As you preached and taught and ministered…

I was there in that sanctified place.

It was I, who watched you go

from the pulpit…

to the depths of hell all in the same day!

Awwwwww but

I am

the Forgiver, your Redeemer…

turn from your wicked ways I say!

OH CHILDREN UNDER THE SOUND OF MY VOICE!

Believe!

I AM!

I am

The beginning, the Alpha…the Omega…

I am

The End.

I am

The Revelation.

I AM…

coming again.

Oh my sheep!

I say I AM!

I am

the one who gave you mouth to mouth,

after I rescued you from drowning in that,

pool of vodka.

I am the safety on the trigger that wouldn't unlock brother,

that would have had you…locked up.

I am

My sister- the one that was there that night.

I am

The One who spoke, "PUT DOWN THAT CRACK PIPE!"

"Daughter I am here, follow me…and you will never hurt again."

I AM

The One who will stay with you from the beginning,

…through…

to the very end.

I am, brother

The One that was there that dreadful night.

Have your forgotten… the bullets that rang?

I am, the one that held you in my arms.

Remember the man that fell at your feet?...yet you were unharmed.

I AM

The One that calls you home- *Lady of the Night*.

The money, the men…come to me daughter,

It's alright!

I AM THE SECOND CHANCE GIVER!

I AM HE!

Confess my children that I AM!

and…

I shall not lead you into temptation,

But to everlasting life.

I will deliver you from evil…

For I AM

The Kingdom, and the Power,

and the Glory,

FOREVER.

"The word is near YOU, in your mouth and in you heart

That is the word of faith that which we are preaching.

That if you confess with your mouth Jesus as Lord, and believe in your heart that God raised Him from the dead, you will be saved;

For with the heart a person believes, resulting in righteousness, and with the mouth he confesses, resulting in salvation."

CHAPTER ONE

Saved & S.E.X.Y. - For the Almighty God

Before I became saved I hated the fact that men would call me sexy. The first thing that came to mind when one would say, "Oh girl you are sooooo sexy!" would be, "They just want sex." My philosophy was if a man's first sentence included a word with "sex" in it, it must mean that the only thing on his mind when he noticed me was sex. Needless to say, nine times out of ten, my philosophy was usually correct.

You see I wasn't born in the church, nor was I reared in one. I was more of a wild child to say the least. So hearing the word sexy and having it used to describe me when a man approached would be comparable to a two-edged sword. Although I knew I could use this to my advantage, many times in my heart I knew I didn't want the word "sex" attached to my first impression.

It wasn't until many years after I was introduced to Christ that I realized there was more of a foundation to the word sexy than many people realize. In the beginning of my walk with Christ I was nervous about the first impression I would make in the church and how other Christians would initially perceive me. I knew my heart was pure, however, I had brainwashed myself to believe that being sexy was a horrible appearance that meant I could never be virtuous or taken as a lady. I can recall every morning before I left for church triple checking myself just to be sure I wasn't sending out any wrong signals or the slightest notion that it was my intention to be sexually noticed. It eventually became so bad, at times I would think to myself, "maybe I shouldn't wear my hair this way to church, I don't want women thinking I want their husband. After all, I am a single woman."

Now let's not be mistaken, in everything we must be cognoscente of our appearance and overall impressions we make on people. What I am referring to is a deep rooted insecurity of myself regarding my God given beauty that I suppressed for many years. As I grew stronger in Christ and understood the dynamics of His way, I realized there was a foundation to my beauty and there was an actual relevance to being sexy. The more I allowed God to mold me and teach me how to become and behave as an honorable woman of God, the more I was able to embrace my inner beauty and my sexiness as a saved woman. Colossians 2:6-10 states, "As you therefore have received Christ Jesus the Lord, so walk in Him, rooted and built up in Him and established in faith, as you have been taught, abounding in it with thanksgiving. Beware lest anyone cheat you through philosophy and empty deceit, according to the tradition of men, according to the basic principles of the world, and not according to Christ. For in Him dwells all the fullness of the Godhead bodily; and you are complete in Him, who is the head of all principality and power." Hallelujah.

This scripture alone has brought me to a place, spiritually, where I am assured God's creation of me and my sex appeal has a place in the kingdom. My philosophy didn't matter nor did the traditions of man. All that matters is that we are complete in Christ and that our genuine faith rests on Christ and Him alone.

I want first to share a few definitions to clarify a couple of things that will allow you to better understand where this book is going to take you and what things I feel I must express within it. I believe once you fully comprehend the expression of S.E.X.Y. and how it is used to define women working for the Kingdom in this book, you will then appreciate the word S.E.X.Y.; and if you happen to be like me, you'll embrace it with everything you have as you continue to grow in the Lord letting Him take you to higher dimensions.

Let's first look at the acronym S.E.X.Y. as I would like you to see it used in this book, shall we?

- **S**-*Satisfied*: Made happy or pleased. Gratified to the fullest.
- **E**-*Encouraged*: Inspired with courage, spirit and hope.
- **X**-*Xenoglossia*: Person's knowledge and speaking of a language never studied (Speaking in Tongues while filled with the Holy Spirit). Originated from the Greek word Glossolalian, meaning: *Glossia*- tongues and *lalian*- to speak. *Xeno*- means foreign.
Notable characteristics would be Latter-Day Saints and Pentecostals. See (Acts 2:4-8)
- **Y**-*Yielding*: Surrendering or submitting oneself to another.

So now that I've shared S.E.X.Y. with you let's look it over. Saved & Satisfied. Saved & Encouraged. Saved &

Xenoglossia. Saved & Yielding...in and to the Almighty God! Now I have to give God some praise on this one.

Next, I would like to break down just a few more words so we can all be on one accord:

- **Sexy**- (*adj.*) generally attractive, interesting or appealing.
- **Sex**- (*noun*) the characteristic of being male or female.
- **Sex Appeal**- (*noun*) male or female attractiveness.
- **Virtuous**- (*adj.*) a person who behaves in a moral and correct way, excellent.
- **Moral**- (*noun*) of or relating to principles of right or wrong behavior.

Summing it all up to get a full understanding of this reading in its entirety, I want you to know that having a physical outer attractiveness, or sex appeal that the opposite sex desires, is only half the gift that God has given you.

Being virtuous, having sound morals and using your S.E.X.Y. to bring glory to God should be your ultimate desire. I believe sex appeal is at its greatest when it is complete in Christ.

In this book, I share with you what I've learned and experienced as a single, married and divorced *saved* woman. I share with you women of the Bible described as being sexy (we'll use sexy in the context of the definition above) and how their attractiveness was a blessing of opportunity many times allowing God to be used through them to accomplish and carry out His ultimate plan. We'll discuss the response by men and their weaknesses to sexy women. We'll then go into the proper responses of women in the Bible in addition to the women that used their sexiness to gain ungodly advantages.

Finally, this book will display how to be *Saved and S.E.X.Y.*; How to embrace your beauty and physical appeal in the manner of a virtuous woman whether you are single, married or recently divorced. I am promoting celibacy but also encouraging your preparation to be a gift from God to your husband. Remember, "He who finds a wife finds a good thing, and obtains favor from the Lord." (Proverbs 18:22)

"Because your loving kindness is better

than life,
My lips shall praise You.
Thus I will bless You while I live; I will lift up my hands in Your name.
My soul shall be satisfied as with marrow and fatness, and my mouth shall praise You with joyful lips.
When I remember You on my bed,

I meditate on You in the night watches.
Because You have been my help,
Therefore in the shadow of Your wings I will rejoice.
My soul follows close behind You;
Your right hand upholds me."
Psalm 63:3-8

CHAPTER TWO

Getting to a Place Where Your S.E.X.Y. Can Be Used by God

Once I made up my mind that I would serve the Lord, the next step, yielding to His will, was the toughest part. Of course we all tend to want to do the things we desire to do opposed to, taking instruction, don't we? Naturally, our own mind tells us that there is no malice or intended harm that may result from our own decisions when we are trying to walk on the right path, so therefore we feel as though we are living the way God intended right? This is so far from the truth and as I learned the way of God I began to understand the scripture "And do not be conformed to this world, but be transformed by the renewing of the mind." (Romans 12:2)

I remember in the beginning of my calling I was truly trying to 'work it out' with my walk with Christ. I was going to church and learning the word. I had been baptized in the name of Jesus, and I was hungry!

It was then that things seemed to shift in an unusual way. I was presented with a test that I now know has changed my life forever- the test of S.E.X.Y.

Countless times I met men and received compliments on my appearance and there that old familiar word would return, *sexy*. "Hey miss, you sure are sexy, how are you doing beautiful?" I would cringe, but at the same time telling myself to let go of the stigma and allow God to use you. So that's just what I did. Sounds easy, right? Wrong. You see, the devil is the trickster of all tricksters and he knew just as well, if not better than me, that my walk with Christ was sincere. However, he also knew my weakness…wanting a sound and committed relationship. Now you may be saying, "What's wrong with that?" and I am saying, nothing. If you are Satisfied, Encouraged, Xenoglossia and Yielding to the Almighty God, there will never be anything wrong with wanting a sound and committed relationship. But when you are still allowing your own mind (the devil's playground) to be your dictator there can be many things wrong with this.

Yes- I was letting the stigma go and learning that sex appeal was not necessarily a bad thing. Yes- I finally understood that God created me with a gift to attract the opposite sex to use it to glorify Him and only Him. Yes- I continuously spoke of the good works of God, invited my men friends to church and even shared with them scriptures pertaining to their own lives. I believed I was doing everything right. But where I failed my test, friends, was at the place where the devil manipulated me to believe that each man that was interested in getting to know God and wanting to be in a relationship with me, despite my transformation, was the man God "just may have" blessed me with to be in that relationship I longed for. The devil is definitely clever!

It's so easy to get off track when you're not seeking God first in everything you do. So because I was not completely satisfied and completely yielding to God's Will for my life, I would get trapped in this massive web of lies and deceit over and over again. Men would come and men would go...but only after the devil laughed in my face making me look like yet another fool. The hurt I felt, every single time I failed the same test, was unbearable. I remember thinking if going through the same fire over and over again until you realize that this self-inflicted pain could have been avoided all together, feels this painful, I never want to visit Hell! The greatest comfort came when my heart was reminded I wasn't in Hell and I still had time to get it right; because once in that fiery pit, regardless if you realize your going there could have been avoided, it's too late- there is no coming back. So I thank God for the many chances He gives for us to get ourselves together.

Understand that I am writing this book to encourage you and in doing so I hope to accomplish two things: 1) To inspire you to embrace your S.E.X.Y. as saved and virtuous women and 2) To have you learn from the mistakes I've made and share with you some of the things I've learned in my walk with Christ from my experiences as it relates to the gift of physical attraction and sex appeal.

It was like bumping my head against a brick wall and knowing it would hurt the same every time. There was always that hope in my mind that the next time I tried things would be different. This logic lasted for many years and needless to say I found myself feeling hurt, ashamed, abandoned and lonely more and more with each relationship that ended. The devil played puppet with me very well. In each attempt to secure a relationship, the greater the lies became, the greater the schemes emerged and the greater the pain felt. It was only when I realized the hope was in my mind, and that it was me trying my way, that I decided to STOP.

I remember crying out to God, "God Why…why…" And that's when God answered.

I Cried, God Answered

Actual words answered by God in my time of despair

Me: How deep can this pain go?

God: As deep as the ocean to your soul.

Me: How great is my overwhelming desire to be free?

God: As great as a desert needs a flowing stream.

Me: How far will this burden ride my shoulders, as I stumble along this dry and lonely trail?

God: As far as your feet will carry you and as loud as your voice can yell.

Me: Is there ever an end to this constant struggle You call temporary?

God: It all depends on the seeds sown…to each it may vary.

Me: But tell me this…I thought love covered a multitude of sins. My love must be worth something!

God: Yes, my child worthy it is, but self love amounts to nothing.

Me: Well when I ask what it is I need to do, I get silence and I feel so far away from you.

God: NO. When I answer it's not popular, so you choose to hear what you want to.

Me: But when I try, I give it my all! Lord I get so close, then I stumble and fall.

God: My child, falling is not as important as being in it for the long haul.

Me: How can I continue like this Lord…constantly getting slapped in my face?

God: Great are the afflictions of the righteous, I will bless those at the proper time and place.

Me: These answers seem so vague I can't sleep!

God: No, it's that you're not laying your burdens at my feet.

You see…

My word is alive and my way is easy and light,

But the key to my promise is that you must continue to fight!

My family is great and many are strong.

They've walked through dead valleys and dry seasons singing your same song.

Some have laid down surrendering their soul,

While others decided they weren't going to fight anymore.

Many have been delivered and given rest, while others feel their own will is best.

I said I would never forsake you, I never said I wouldn't observe.

I am waiting patiently for you to wholeheartedly decide who to serve.

I love ALL my children, but remember this one thing…

There is only one way to Heaven and that is through the one born of the King!

Me: Father! Forgive me! I was dwelling in self pity.

I will get up now and continue to speak Your Word from city to city.

I do thank you Lord for your forgiveness and showing me the right way.

I thank you for speaking to me and through me today.

As I close, I pray for all that may be weak.

Please hold them close, I ask their hearts that you keep.

For I know Lord my prayer today is the prayer of many

…But I am also convinced and able to say your love is plenty.

So I have dried my tears and picked up my cross.

I'm moving on!

ONCE AGAIN DEVIL YOU'VE LOST!

God told me that once I surrendered my way to His, things would shift in my favor. He explained that he had sent many men to me, not for relationships, but to plant a seed of faith in them. He was using me for His purpose and I was allowing the devil to use me also to discredit everything God was trying to do in my life. God allowed me to see that the gift of sex appeal He has given me was only to attract initially, and forever allow Him to use me thereafter. He promised me if I followed His instruction and became a living witness of how God can turn my situation around; He would lead me out of bondage. He offered rest, an end to my pain, and assured me I would never feel abandoned or lonely again.

I believe weariness causes you to search far beyond a valley for rest. I also believe pain can force any creature to call out for aid higher than any mountain top. Even more so, I believe God will bring healing and restoration to any situation if you allow Him to.

"Come to Me, all you who labor and are heavy laden, and I will give you rest. Take My yoke upon you and learn from Me, for I am gentle and lowly in heart, and you will find rest for your souls. For My yoke is easy and My burden is light"

Matthew 11:28-30

CHAPTER THREE

S.E.X.Y. Women in the Bible

When we think about women who are *Saved & S.E.X.Y. for the Almighty God*, we tend to search the Bible for women we can relate to. There are undoubtedly numerous women Christ chose to use throughout the Bible as witnesses. Because so many women played such significant and active roles in the church in the Old and New Testament, they brought glory to God by ways of evangelism, prophecy, teaching and discipleship. Now I'm going to take a random guess with this, but I'm pretty sure all the women God used to bring Glory to the Kingdom weren't unattractive creatures.

Let's take Sarah (Sarai) for instance (Genesis 12:11-20). One distinctive characteristic the Bible reveals about Sarah is her beauty. The Bible states Sarah's beauty was so overwhelming that her husband Abraham (Abram) knew the Egyptians would kill him if they knew she was his wife. So therefore, he asked Sarah to lie to the Pharaoh's Officials and say she was his sister. This is a prime example of how a man can allow a woman's sex appeal to cloud his best judgment and his trust in God. Out of fear that another man's attraction for his beautiful wife would slay him, Abraham chose to forsake his God to satisfy his own desire. Because of Sarah's submissiveness and faithfulness to her husband she agreed to go along with his lie. The struggle was Sarah knew God and as the Bible states she failed several times when it came to trusting in Him wholeheartedly. Needless to say, this is what many of us do, constantly, regardless of gender.

When we do not totally trust God and His promise we tend to make bad choices instead of trusting God all the way. I found it extremely difficult at times to put my total trust in God just like Sarah because so many people had disappointed me in the past. I knew I loved God yet at times when faced with split decisions, there seemed to be no other way but the way of my own decision. Therefore the end result always led to disaster.

I remember when I finally made up my mind to trust God with everything I had no matter what the present looked like or what I was *foretold* the end result would be, I was faced with a job loss, a mortgage, a car note, two children and a dog to care for and it had been trial after trial that I had failed the same test to put my trust in God wholeheartedly. I recall praying to God, "Father, I have nothing to lose, but everything to gain if I can just fear not and totally allow You to provide for my family through this difficult time. It's not that I don't know Your power it's that it's extremely difficult to just lay this situation down at the alter and walk away. It's like being blind folded and falling backwards hoping the person is there to catch you. God, here it is…I'm putting my total trust in You. My heart is weak but I know that you are strong. I trust You."

With that confession, there was a transformation. God stepped in and my finances didn't skip a beat! Every dart the devil threw during that time God blocked it. Yes, He is a faithful God. I learned from this experience and many others that yielding to the Almighty God and resting in Him is always going to work out for your good.

1Samuel 25 talks about a woman named Abigail, another woman who was *Saved & S.E.X.Y. for the Almighty God*. Abigail is one of my favorite women in the Bible to read about. It's reported that Abigail was a woman of great beauty and intelligence whose wisdom and leadership saved her entire family from being destroyed. Her courageous act of humbling herself, first before God and then before David, proved her yielding spirit resulted in great success. The Book also tells us that Abigail was so attractive that when God struck Nabal, Abigail's wicked husband, dead; David who was overwhelmingly intrigued with her sex appeal, wanted to take Abigail as his own and sent his servants to ask Abigail to become his wife.

Please remember the women I am describing were more than just attractive or sexually appealing. Each woman of God played a vital role in God's plan. Their sex appeal was great – yes; however their love for God, their submissiveness and their modest nature honored God. I had to learn, as many of you have had or will have to learn how to become humble, and balance physical attributes and sex appeal so that it glorifies and does not dishonor God. This lesson learned will be an *everlasting-life* long gain.

This balance is extremely important. It proves true for those of you who are raising young girls as well. Teaching your girls that their outer appearance and attitude should be met with Godly service and humility so that they will be appreciated and rewarded for their good works and not strictly on sex appeal should be priority.

The Story of Rebekah is an excellent example (Genesis 24:15-28). Rebekah's services to the servants of Abraham were that in which God wants us to perform. When Rebekah offered water to the servant and his camels (offering water to the camels was significant), she was rewarded with jewels and gold and asked to be Isaac's (son of Abraham) wife. God blesses those who honor Him. God blessed Rebekah with a husband that truly loved and cherished her for many years to come.

I can go on and on about sexy women in the Bible. Although I believe my point has been made regarding the balance we have to hold steadily in our lives concerning our sex appeal and our walk with God, I want to discuss one other woman I found to be more than just sexy, but extraordinary in all her ways. This woman is Queen Esther.

Queen Esther (Book of Esther) was extremely beautiful and sexy. So intriguing to the eye that Esther was entered in a beauty contest. Esther and many other women who sought to become the King's wife had prepared for twelve months prior to being chosen by the king. The book says she was so appealing that even the King's custodian showed favor upon her and put her in a special place in the palace for women who are to prepare themselves to be wives of the King. Esther's sexy opened up doors of opportunity that may have never been presented if she would not have used her sex appeal (even though without much effort) to her advantage.

Esther was chosen to be King Ahasuerus's wife solely because of her beauty, but the book goes on to show us that Esther was faced with an overwhelming challenge that could have resulted in her people (Jews) being destroyed. But Esther prayed and began fasting allowing God to use her even if it meant that her own life would be taken. The story goes on to say Esther succeed in her attempt to save her people; Ultimately, respected and honored by the King and the people of the land, she had the privilege of re-writing the law and to this day Queen Esther is honored every year during the Jewish Holiday "Purim" for her courage and success in saving the Jewish people who resided in the land.

So because Esther trusted and allowed God to order her steps in every situation, she's yet another S.E.X.Y. woman God glorified for her faithfulness.

"Blessed be the God and Father of our Lord Jesus Christ, the Father of mercies and God of all that we may be able to comfort those who are in any trouble, with the comfort with which we ourselves are comforted by God."

2 Corinthians 1:3-4

CHAPTER FOUR

Living Saved & S.E.X.Y. Single

Like many women, I wasn't always saved. Now I know there are some that were raised in the church and may not have one story to share to someone that is coming out of a worldly situation. I also, know there are going to be some women that do not want to share their stories due to shame. That's okay too. My motto has always been ever since I could remember making sense to myself- If you're going to be ashamed of anything that you decide to do, don't do it. This saying has actually taken me an extremely long way. Many times I've had to talk myself out of certain situations with this saying which has saved me from a few potentially humiliating outcomes. Through the years I've relied on many of my own inner spirit voices to guide me. At least that's what I would call them before I was saved. I've always known I had something there all along guiding me, molding me and protecting me along my way. Now that I look back on the divine interventions that I'd constantly encountered and how each one had brought me to the place I am in my life now, I get overjoyed knowing that God was there all along!

I laugh every time someone looks at me in amazement when I tell them a story about my past. The usual response is, "I would of never thought you would have done that..." or "Wow, you seem so different now..." I'm sure if you ask a few of my close knit female friends who knew my before and after Glamour Shot Photo in Christ, they'd have plenty to tell for you to bargain for. After all, I've always been sexy and single, but I wasn't always *Saved and S.E.X.Y.*

Oh the partying! The night clubs! The all night hang-outs, the men! I was single, young and free! I refuse to lie to you and say I didn't enjoy those years, because I did. Those years were some of the best and some of the worst years of my life. Naturally, I have many more to experience, Lord's

Will, but I truly learned several things about conforming to a world of sex, drugs, partying and lies. I am actually thankful that I've lived it and made it through to tell the story.

As I mentioned, I was extremely insecure about the initial impressions I made on men. If you missed that chapter, it wasn't because I didn't find myself appealing, but that I didn't want men to find me sexually appealing. I would be offended at the thought of a man expressing that he found me sexy. I eventually came to realize those were hidden insecurities I had that would not be overcome until I was whole in Christ. I was never a woman to "use what I got to get what I want or even needed." If you happen to be this woman, I have something in here for you too.

The type of woman I was, however, was the type that searched for love in all the wrong places. A hopeless lover is what some would call it. You see, I believed there was love out there just waiting to saturate my heart with a love that was indescribable. The problem was I just didn't know exactly where or who it was that was to love me like this. So I started as a young women searching. I dated big time drug dealers, college men, business owners, preacher's sons, gang bangers, military men, school teachers, policemen, ministers, pastors and just some good old momma's boys. I have dated, gotten accustomed to each environment, learned each mannerism and have taken something with me from each one of those relationships. I've definitely had my share to choose from and I have utilized all my resources if I do say so myself. Now some of you may read this and cringe at some of the expressions I use within this book. That's ok, I understand. Just keep reading.

Yeah those years were fun, but at what cost? I searched and searched for years. In each man I looked for the light at the end of the tunnel. I wondered every time, "Is this going to be that love I believe in?" and every time I was disappointed. I was more disappointed in the outcome more so than the men I would date or the added number to my list of partners. Each man had his own story to tell. And with each encounter there was a new lesson to be learned. It wasn't until much later in life, after I had become saved that I became extremely disappointed with myself as I looked back at each man that came in and out of my life and in and out of my bed through the years. Now this isn't a Juanita Bynum moment, when she ministers her "No More Sheets" message. By the way if you haven't had a chance to hear that message, please look it up- It's phenomenal. No, I was disappointed in myself because I realized that all those years of me being single and building trust and friendships with so many different types of men, I could have been ministering to these men and introducing them to Christ. Yes, each relationship initially started with "sexy," but each could have ended up with a seed planted and using my sex appeal to my advantage to win souls for the Kingdom while saving myself for the man God hand picked for me opposed to me picking. Instead, Satan had me fooled. He had me prancing around in the dark looking for something that didn't exist in man. Everything I gave in those relationships didn't benefit me or the man. I say didn't benefit either of us because I am speaking now in the super natural and not the physical. This only benefited Satan. "For our struggle is not against flesh and blood, but against the rulers, against the authorities, against the powers of this dark world and against the spiritual forces of evil in the heavenly realms." (Ephesians 6:12)

Satan knew the calling God had on my life from the start, just as he knows the calling God has on yours. If you don't take anything away from this book, please take this: Satan has watched you from the time you were brought into this world. He knows your first steps, your first words and your first school day. He is aware of your family secrets, your first love, your first pain, your insecurities and your weaknesses. Oh yes, he knows. He is tricky, clever and he's the manipulator of all manipulators. Believe me when I tell you, without Christ, you will not beat him! Do not fall for the enemy's plot to have your body, mind and spirit used and abused over and over again. He knows you're searching, he knows your longing and hoping and he will do whatever it takes and whoever it takes to chew you up and spit you out!

Now that I am *Saved and S.E.X.Y.*, I am definitely Satisfied, Encouraged, Xenoglossia and Yielding to and in the Almighty God! I know now that each man that smiles and compliments my sexy just may not be the "one." I've learned how to seek God first in everything I do and I can testify to you that He will lead you, guide you and reveal to you His plan in each situation. Friends, you must be married to Christ while living single, submitting to Him first. Know God so that you will be able to recognize who is and who is not of Him. Men are going to come into your life, some are simple connections, or should I say destiny needs you to transition them to the place in which God's plan has them aligned. Others are going to be assignments for you to either, teach, share or learn from. And many will be tests to take you to higher dimensions in Christ. Don't fail these tests. Trust God's instruction in every situation and you will be victorious.

Once I understood my sexy, I allowed God to lead my life and said goodbye to the world, all my insecurities left. I began to embrace my sex appeal, accepting it as a gift of opportunity. I wrapped it up, packaged it and prepared myself to use it the way Christ intended it to be used. There wasn't anymore searching for that love I believed was out there, because I had found it- It was there with me all along. It was that inner spirit voice I heard telling me never to do anything I would be ashamed of, it was that hope I held on to that there was a love out there just waiting to saturate my heart… it was Christ. He welcomed me with opened arms and as the saying goes "a woman's heart should be so hidden in Christ a man must seek Him first to find her." I am so grateful for His love.

"O God,

You are my God;
Early will I seek You;
My soul thirsts for You;
My flesh longs for You in a dry and thirsty land
Where there is no water.
So I have looked for You in the sanctuary,
To see Your power and glory.
Because Your loving-kindness is better than life,
My lips shall praise You.
Thus I will bless You while I live; I will lift up my hands in Your name.
My soul shall be satisfied as with marrow and fatness.
And my mouth shall praise You with joyful lips."

Psalm 63:1-5

CHAPTER FIVE

Living S.E.X.Y. & Married, S.E.X.Y. & Divorced

I'm always looking back on my life and thanking God for the experiences I've been through whether they've been good or bad. Being married was one experience I can say I've definitely learned a lot from. Not only can I contribute my patience for the opposite sex to being married, I can also contribute many passed and failed tests to it as well. I wasn't at all where I am today when I was married, nor was my ex-husband where he could have been in Christ. However, I can say that one important element of being married that should never falter, is being sure your S.E.X.Y. never leaves.

Being married and saved is phenomenal, but being married, saved and sexy should never be compromised. I learned to stay beautiful for my husband, never allowing myself to get totally physically out of hand with the woman he fell in love with. Now don't get me wrong, staying attractive took on a whole different meaning to me for a very long time. Even during the time I was searching and seeking God within my marriage. I had to learn that being sexually appealing to my husband didn't mean wearing revealing and tasteless clothing (1Timothy 2:9 God commands us to dress modestly) nor did it mean bringing attention to myself from everyone outside of my marriage. It didn't mean for me not to be submissive to my husband's wishes or desires when it came to a change he may want to see. By no means should you ever compromise your salvation and the commandments of God whether it be for your husband or anyone else. I learned through Christ staying attractive for my husband did mean however, keeping myself interesting and trying to express the same appeal to my husband that I expressed when we were dating. After all, we tend to fall in love with one thing, and so it's only fair that we all work hard not to let that one thing change into another before time insists, right? Yes it's true, being saved will illuminate from the inside, making you absolutely beautiful on the outside as well. I remember God speaking to me saying it is not the attention to the outer sexy that will win a husband, Tiffany, but the inner S.E.X.Y. that will when his soul.

Naturally, something didn't quite work out the way things were intended, because I am now divorced and single once again. God has a strange way of teaching us His way through trials and tribulations, doesn't He? Like thousands of others, after I was divorced I felt as though I had failed at something. Depression set in briefly with self doubt and fears about the future. I knew I was a saved wife, wasn't I? Well, I can honestly say my walk definitely was not where it should have been or where it is today. So for that, I thank God even for the experience of divorce. It allowed me to wholeheartedly trust and depend on HIM. My S.E.X.Y. kicked in full force and I was able to praise God even in the middle of that whirlwind of emotions that divorcees go through, placing both my feet firmly on leveled ground allowing God to finally take full control over my life. Yes, I yielded to the Almighty God! I realized that even within a marriage we have to be married to Christ first and foremost or it will not work.

After divorce I was a bit apprehensive about being single again. Because I was "back on the market," it was only a matter of time before I would start dating again. I joined an online chat room and a couple of social groups. I met a few new friends and a couple of interesting men in addition to being introduced to a few men through co-workers and friends. I went on several dates and a few dates turned into interests, while a couple of those interests turned into potential relationships. Sounds easy, right? Wrong. I realized quickly that the same dating policy and procedures that were in place before I had been married were not applicable these days. There were new games, new schemes and rules! I was out in a world I had no clue about. Saved and single in a world that I didn't belong in; "Do not be conformed to this world but be transformed by the renewing of your mind." (Romans 2:12) I'm going to tell you, I had to take a big step back! I had to regroup and refocus.

I recall one night I was so fed up with the way I was being mistreated and gamed upon over and over. I was exhausted from driving down dead-end roads and it seemed as though the pain was affecting my job and my family…not to mention it was tearing me up inside. I started to feel like I was losing myself to the world. Where had my self-esteem gone? I was settling for behaviors and characteristics in men that I had never allowed before. Had

I resorted to this? Letting anyone into my life and allowing people to misuse and emotional abuse me? Where was my S.E.X.Y.?

That night was a turning point in my life. I had just broken up with a man I was engaged to who I loved and I truly thought loved me- a saved man. I thought I had done everything right. Saved myself, cooked, cleaned, had been patient, prayed, all of those things I felt were required of me being a Christian woman. Now that I look back, I realized there were several things I did wrong. One, I prayed for answers, but didn't receive the answers given. Another, I didn't trust God to remove all things and all people from my life in fear I would be alone. I allowed confusion to control my mind, "For God has not given us a spirit of fear, but of power and of love and of a sound mind." (2Timothy 1:7) But the most important thing I now understand is that you can not proclaim that you are Satisfied, Encouraged, Xenoglossia and Yielding to the Almighty God if you are not allowing yourself to be led by the Spirit.

I walked in my bedroom that night totally broken. I was shaking and on the verge of a nervous breakdown. I just fell to the floor and cried out to God, "God I can't take this pain anymore…please Jesus help me! Oh God please help me…I don't want to live like this…isn't there someone out there that loves You enough to love me! Jesus please take the hurt away…"

In the middle of my despair, God came down and embraced me that night and I have never been the same.

The Bible tells us in Colossians 2:6-7, "Therefore as you have received Christ Jesus the Lord, so walk in Him. Having been firmly rooted and now being built up in Him and established, and overflowing with gratitude."

Through much pain and rebirthing, I've definitely learned a lot. The best advice I can give is to be aware of the enemy's death sentence for your life. Seek God's face constantly as you live as a single woman or a single woman with marriage experiences! Again remember the world is the devil's playground and he loves it when the innocent are set free; in my case- a saved, recently divorced, vulnerable and lonely woman who had been set free. I was like a sheep in the middle of a pack of wolves, but God taught me that "Ye though I walk in the shadow of death, I shall fear no evil, for He is with me."

Always keep in mind the devil and his hell angels have strategically set out to destroy who we are as virtuous women and will do anything possible to play against our loneliness. During the process of separation and divorce is the best time for the enemy to attack because just getting out of a marriage, most are accustomed to having sex and companionship on a regular basis. Allow yourself time to heal, allow yourself time with God to strengthen you as a single woman again. Get yourself prepared once again to become a gift from God. If you desire to be remarried, be cautious that your motives are correct and any bitterness or anger is gone.

Some may not want to be remarried which is just fine, but the appeal should still be there. Our walk as *Saved and S.E.X.Y.* women should be natural and illuminate with every step we take!

"Father, I desire that they also whom You gave Me may be with Me where I am, that they may behold My glory which You have given Me; for You loved me before the foundation of the world. O righteous Father!

The world has not known you, but I have known You; and these have known that You sent Me.

And I have declared to them Your name, and will declare it, that the love with which You loved Me may be in them, and I in them."

CHAPTER SIX

Saved, S.E.X.Y.

&

Honorable in This World

Let's remember there are many people watching you and many more that may want to model who and what you stand for. Keep in mind the Glory belongs to God. It's easy to become vain and self absorbed, but a true woman of God will always stay humble and meek, kind and loving, giving and quick to look to the hill! Continue to be led by the Spirit opposed to the flesh. There is only one way the flesh will lead you and that is to your grave.

There is significance in why women have a certain sex appeal. Biblical history has proven the fact that there are just some people that are drawn to an attractive woman. In addition, there are some that will not pay attention to anything you attempt to share with them unless the visual is interesting as well. Men are visual creatures first. God knows this and I believe that in everything God has a place. It's time to get about our Father's business ladies and stop putting limitations on God through religion and bondage! Our Lord has no limits yet we put our own limits on God's interventions; Failing to remember His historically demonstrated power, signs and use of various people. It's not what is on the outside as we are constantly reminded, but truly what is on the inside. We must bear fruit in order to be fruitful. God tells us, "I am the vine; you are the branches. If a man remains in Me and I in him, he will bear much fruit; but apart from Me you can do nothing." (John 15:5)

Ministering and sharing the good Word of the Lord should be our first and main objective. I've learned that living with a physical attractiveness or sex appeal can be a blessing and curse. It's much easier now that I've put my flesh under subjection and I know who I am in Christ. I won't lie, it took many years of searching for the truth. I visited many churches that celebrated only limited gifts God gives us, and I failed numerous tests before I concluded that God's gift of attraction is to draw people to Him through us. **God instructs us "not to let our behavior be** like that of this world, but be changed and made new in our mind, so that by experience we may have knowledge of the good and pleasing and complete purpose of Him." (Romans 12:2) We are to conduct ourselves honorably among the world, so they will observe our good works. We are to sow seeds, and as scripture states, "you shall reap what you sow."

Of course this does not pertain solely to attracting men with your sexy; this includes women and men, young and old alike. Why? Because I have noticed there are many women wanting to release their sexy, but unfortunately they have been brainwashed to believe that their God given sex appeal and gift of attractiveness is to be packed away, locked and the key thrown away. They are intimidated and or afraid because of the stigma that the Christian society has put on the word sex appeal. Ladies, get you together. Look in the mirror and unleash your natural beauty God has gifted you with! Ask God what it is HE wants you to look like, act like and present yourself like so that you will work to your fullest ability for His Kingdom. If you have to pull out those pumps and put on a power suit for God to get out there to minister to the business world, ladies, let your hair down and get picture perfect! God is calling all women who are *Saved & S.E.X.Y. for the Almighty God.* Prepare yourself as the women of the Bible did. Know that you have more to offer than your beauty, but be wise not to allow your insecurities to hinder opportunities for God.

I've gotten women in and out the church, ministers, pastors and even seasoned saints, complimenting me or commenting on my demeanor and my sex appeal. On the other hand, I've been misunderstood, judged, lied on, talked about and deliberately shut out due to my overall disposition. Not because of my actions or my attitude, but because some people do not accept what's not familiar or popular. In other cases, some may have been intimidated or envious at the fact that many of us are embracing our attractiveness these days, thus causing controversy right now with being *Saved & S.E.X.Y. for the Almighty God.*

The world, unfortunately, works this way. Sadly it's probably in some of your churches as well. Until we get on the ball, we'll be stuck with limited methods of trying to win souls for Christ. Your sexy does not have to be a hindrance, it must be packaged and respected and utilized in a way that it ultimately brings people closer to God. Of course there will be opposition to the word "sexy"- many may even call it an oxymoron, but let's stop allowing society's erroneous perspective of God's limitations of our gifts to keep us from being all we can be in the Lord.

"Be hospitable to one another without grumbling. As each one has received a gift, minister it to one another, as good stewards of the manifold grace of God. If anyone speaks, let him speak as the oracles of God. If anyone ministers, let him do it as with the ability which God supplies, that in all things God may be glorified through Jesus Christ, to whom belong the glory and the dominion forever and ever Amen." (1Peter 4:9-11)

Yes, my friends, having sex appeal is only half the battle, but when you allow God to use you and you become S.E.X.Y. for the Almighty God, you will be victorious!

May God bless you and keep you.

*"Judge me, O Lord, according to my righteousness, and according to my integrity within me.
Oh let the wickedness of the wicked come to an end,
But establish the just;
For the righteous God tests the hearts and minds.
My defense is of God,
Who saves the upright in heart."
Psalm 7:8-10*

Daily Prayers and Dedications

The more I desired to do more for God, I decided to add spiritual meaning to everyday of the week. Understanding that walking with Him everyday is an important breakthrough in our spiritual journey. It's one thing to pray in the morning, over your meals and right before you lay your head down in the evening to sleep; but it's another thing to dedicate each day to God. Making each day a contribution to God will bring forth an overwhelming response; casting down all plans the enemy has for your life or your love ones' lives for that day. It adds to the well known scripture, "No weapon formed against me shall prosper." (Isaiah 54:17) Scripture states, "If you abide in Me, and My words abide in you, ask whatever you wish and it will be done for you. My Father is glorified by this, that you bear much fruit, and *so* prove to be my disciples." (John 15:1-8)

So I started my *Saved and S.E.X.Y.* Daily Dedications trusting God's promise. Each day of the week has a catchy title to it that I share with all my friends, co-workers and anyone that I think may need an encouraging word or a hope-filled day. Speaking from experience when you start your day off with Him, things go so much better!

Originally, I created a distribution list with a close circle of friends and family to send out the Daily Dedications. Soon, I began receiving reply emails from people I didn't know saying how blessed they were to have read the dedications. Then, the list became massive. You may use these on the job, in your home or church, or in your own way. The whole objective is to take each day and make it about God.

> I get so happy when my circle of friends share their testimonies and then their circle of friends start to share their testimonies, and so on. Soon the day becomes a day of meaning and overwhelming joy.

Motivation Monday-

I like to thank God for the start of a new week. I motivate myself to encourage others to get motivated for Him as well. I begin to think of the challenges that God has assured us will come and I get prepared to fight the battle yet again. Get excited about the works of the Lord! Praise God in advance for protecting you and your family throughout the week. Dedicate the week to Him and inspire others to do the same. Grab a scripture early in the morning and meditate on it throughout the day. Share what you've read with others; you never know- this may be the only time some people actually hear a Word from the Lord. Keep in mind, you're a vessel to be used by God and your mission is to encourage and give others hope through the teachings of Jesus Christ our Lord and Savior.

And if all else fails, Motivation Monday should be used to just simply encourage yourself!

~Prayer~

Lord,

thank You for the beginning of a new week. I dedicated this week to You and welcome You into it. I declare today Motivation Monday and I am motivated for You God! I ask that You be the leader of my day and the watchman over my night this week. I ask Father that You minister to my spirit as I encourage and minister others today. I know I have a work to do Jesus on this earth. I thank You in advance that no hand that rises up against me while I do the work of the Kingdom prevails. I'm thanking You in advance that my eyes and ears are open to any plot that walks or whispers. I praise You today Lord! I thank You this Monday that Your Will be done. I praise You this Monday that I am better today than I was yesterday. I praise You today that I am stronger than I was last week…and I praise You this Monday Lord that I am able to walk in Your grace and that I am **S**aved & **S**atisfied, **E**ncouraged, **X**enoglossia and **Y**ielding for the Almighty God. As I close Father, I ask that anything that I have done to upset or offend anyone be revealed. I ask that my attitude doesn't hinder any answers or blessings You have for my situation this week; and I ask that I am equipped to make a spiritual difference in someone's life this week, as I bring glory and honor to You.

> Get excited about the works of the Lord! Praise God in advance for protecting you and your family throughout the week. Dedicate the week to Him and inspire others to do the same.

Testimony Tuesday-

I love testimony Tuesdays because it gives me a chance to brag on my Father and just dedicate this day to sharing God's kindness and mercies with everyone and anyone who is hungry or hoping for my testimony to bless their situation. I get so happy when my circle of friends share their testimonies and then their circle of friends start to share their testimonies, and so on. Soon the day becomes a day of meaning and overwhelming joy.

Share your story. Tell others how good God is and how good He's been. There should always be something you want to share with others regarding the goodness of God. If you can't think of something for that particular week, think back and remember where God's brought you from. Always remember it's from us looking back on our lives when we get the strength to continue to push forward.

~Prayer~

Lord,

I remember when...(*your testimony*). I am so blessed to be a part of Your family. I'm sharing this story with others this Tuesday to bring honor to You in faith that my testimony will bring someone else into a sense of peace for their own personal situation. For Your Word says, "Let the redeemed of the Lord say so, whom He has redeemed from the hand of the enemy." (Psalm 107:1-2) So "I will tell of what You have done for my soul!" (Psalm 66:16) I declare today Testimony Tuesday and as I spread the Good News with everyone on my distribution list and the people I come in contact with, I pray the spirit rests upon them as well encouraging them to share their stories.

Worthy Wednesday-

This is one of my favorite days of the week. Because it's the middle of a work week and usually called "hump day." This day I declared as Worthy Wednesday because God is so worthy to be praised even in the middle of the hardest day of the week we should still have peace in our spirits with knowing God is with us. I tend to focus on worship and study more on this day. If you choose to fast once a week, Wednesday may be the day for this as well.

Speak life and strength into your day and continue to prove to others that God is worthy with scripture, fasting and prayer…Get exited!

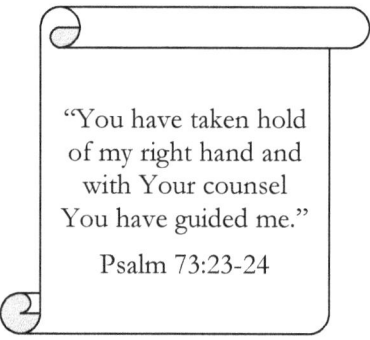

"You have taken hold of my right hand and with Your counsel You have guided me."

Psalm 73:23-24

~Prayer~

Lord,

You are so worthy this Wednesday to be praised. My heart leaps at thought of the Heavens opening and pouring blessings on Your people. "How blessed is the man who has made the Lord his trust." (Psalm 40:4) "Many, Oh Lord are the wonders which You have done, and Your thoughts toward me; there is none to compare with You. If I would try and declare and speak of them, they'd be too numerous to count." (Psalm 40:5) Father You have answered me throughout this week from Your holy heaven and have stayed close to me. You are worthy of worship and praise! You've been my help and have spared me from the enemy's mouth! I exalt Your name today Lord. "You have taken hold of my right hand and with Your counsel You have guided me." (Psalm 73:23-24) You have protected me this week and permitted no man to oppress me. So for this and so much more Father, You are Worthy to be praised!

Thankful Thursday-

On this day I love to just focus on thanking God and just reflect. I continuously remind myself and others how God saves and how thankful we all should be to have a Savior such as Him. He strengthens and sustains, and for this we all should be so thankful.

Get it in your Spirit and heart to give wholeheartedly to Him everyday. You'll feel renewed and cleansed. Starting off with thanks will always turn into a joyous praise!

~Prayer~

Lord,

I thank You this Thursday for making crooked roads straight and seemingly unattainable goals right in arms reach for me. I thank You for the Word to stand on, Your teachings to live by and Your Spirit which dwells in me. I thank You today Father! Today I enter into Your presence with song in my heart and thanksgiving as my Spirit rejoices over all that You've bestowed upon me. You are a righteous and just God and I thank You for destroying all my enemies as they stepped and are stepping in my path this week God. I thank You for being my refuge in times of despair and my counselor in times of confusion. Because of You God, I am sustained. I am **S**atisfied, **E**ncouraged, **X**enoglossia and **Y**ielding this week. Thank You Father. Thank You for giving me an unimaginable peace. I bless and glorify Your name above all names Jesus. You lived Jesus, You died and Jesus You've risen. "Let the words of my mouth and the meditation of my heart as I give thanks to You be acceptable in Your sight, most gracious God," as my heart continues throughout this day to sing a song of thanks.

> Get it in your Spirit and heart to give wholeheartedly to Him everyday. You'll feel. renewed and cleansed Starting off with thanks will always turn into a joyous praise!

Faithful Friday -

YES! I made it through the work week! Thank you Jesus! "I can do all things through Christ, who strengthens me." (Philippians 4:13) Your Word is Faithful and true. You will take care of your own! God is a man that will not lie…and His Word is alive and true yesterday, today and forevermore.

When we feel low or uncertain, God is always right there to lift and assure us that we are His. He promised us He would see us through until the end and we must give thanks with a grateful heart that He is faithful in all that He says He will do. Because a peaceful end to a work week is uncertain, yet always hoped for, just know that when God is with you daily that last day brings on so much gratitude! We realize what our week actually could have ended on worse terms and again we rejoice when we think of how faithful our Father has been.

~Prayer~

Lord,

As this work week comes to a close, I thank You for Your faithfulness. You have seen me through every day this week. Because of Your grace and protection, my family is well. Peace has surpassed all understanding of this from Monday morning until now and Your Word has proven to be true once again. You have been faithful Father in every Word and promise that has come out of Your mouth. Every Word You've sent out this week for my life has not come back void, for You are God! I just ask Father as I continue on my journey this Friday, my head be anointed. I trust in Your protection and guidance today that all will end well today on earth, as it ends well every day in Heaven. I have hope and assurance that You are my Jehovah- Jireh! I understand the devil knows this Friday is the end of yet another battle so he and his hell angels are busy planning attacks on my life and my family's life; But ye though I walk in the valley of the shadow of death, I will fear NO evil for Thou are with me. You remind us that without faith it is impossible to please You. This Friday I have a renewed faith and a grateful heart that You are always faithful to me.

> When we feel low or uncertain, God is always right there to lift and assure us that we are His. He promised us He would see us through until the end and we must give thanks with a grateful heart that He is faithful in all that He says He will do.

Saved Saturday-

"God I am *Saved and S.E.X.Y.* and I will walk this Saturday anointed and appointed!" Remember *who you are* as you are enjoying your weekend. Not just on the days that you travel to and from work or are caught up in your daily routine. Saturday is usually a day for fun and sun or just to let your hair down. We lose sight at times when we are relaxed and socializing with old friends or family now that we have been called new creatures in Christ. We are to influence and not to be influenced. It's easy to get of track so pick up your cross even on Saturday and start your day. Remember, God has also created your leisure day to glorify Him as well. Even in your recreation, remember you are saved.

~Prayer~

Lord,

You are my strength and my Redeemer. Cleanse me from secret faults God and deliver me from my presumptuous sins today. I want to walk upright in Your sight and not fall back into this world of misfortune and deceit. God I come to You in Spirit, with my concerns for this Saturday *(call out all your concerns, struggles, weaknesses)*. I confess these things to You God asking that my insecurities and fears, as I go through this day, be met with Your rod and staff. May Your grace follow me today. I will not be ashamed nor overtaken, for I trust in You God.

> We are to influence and not to be influenced. It's easy to get of track so pick up your cross even on Saturday and start your day.

Satisfied Sunday-

Sundays are a great time to fellowship and receive good teaching. It should be a day that your spirit is filled, and hope restored. Sunday is the day that God's instruction for your life should remind you that our purpose rests in Him. As you begin your Sunday, your attitude should be scrutinized and your mind should be set. You should be ready to receive every teaching, every correction, every answer and every reward the Holy Spirit has for you. This is why it is so important to get involved in and attend an honest, Spirit-filled, loving and dedicated church.

Declare Sunday Sanctified out of your mouth. You want to be totally filled with the Holy Spirit and satisfied with your portion!

~Prayer~

Lord,

This Sunday I open my heart to Your Word. I welcome You into this body and give You total authority. Use me this Sunday as I fellowship and socialize. I want to be more like You God. Let the teaching of today fill my mouth so that I can carry it out into the world. I want to be a doer of Your Word and not just a listener. I ask that anything that may block me from receiving what You have for my spirit today be cast down. I want to be led by Your Spirit, being fruitful as I declare today Sanctified Sunday. Father I come to You today seeking counsel on *(what it is you may need guidance in)*. I need to hear from You God. Your Word says You will not leave me wandering in the dark nor will You ever forsake Your children. So I thank You now for what I am about to receive! Bless Your name God! The one who sits High up in the Heavens. You are the Almighty God! Glory be to Your name.

"So will My word be which goes forth from My mouth; It will not return to Me empty, Without accomplishing what I desire and without succeeding in the matter for which I sent it. For you will go out with joy And be led forth with peace."
Isaiah 55: 11-12

www.ingramcontent.com/pod-product-compliance
Lightning Source LLC
LaVergne TN
LVHW010344260326
834688LV00036B/875